otherwise, it will cause interference with the other electronic appliances.

3. Now plug the adapter into the wall socket and the other end with the Echo's power socket.

4. Now Echo's light will glow blue before turning orange. At this time Alexa will Welcome you with greetings.

Connecting to Wi-Fi

1. Open the Alexa Apps
2. Now open the left-hand-side navigation panel
3. Go to 'Settings' from the options
4. Now select your device and Select 'Set up a new device
5. Now press the 'Action' button for 5 seconds, this will change the light of the Light Ring to orange.
6. Now go to the Alexa Apps, you will

see the list of wifl networks available to be connected, Now select your network and type in your password to connect.

## Choosing your wake word

Before you start using Alexa, you need to choose your wake word, the wake word is how Alexa knows you need something.

By default, the Echo responds to the word "Alexa" or "Echo" but you want to change your wake up word then you need to follow the following steps.

1. Open the Alexa Apps
2. Go to left-hand side navigation panel.
3. Select "Settings"
4. Now choose your device.

5. Go to the "Options"
6. Now select "wake word' from the drop down menu choose your wake word.
7. Now the light will flash orange for seconds.

**Light Ring:**

The light has several meanings by which the Echo communicates visually to you.

Echo will visually display Alexa's status, Following is the list of light ring codes-

**Color**
    **Meaning**

Solid blue with
    Echo is starting

spinning cyan
light

All lights
    Echo is active and
ready for request
off

Orange light spinning
        Connecting to wifi
in a clockwise direction

Oscillating violet
light
    Error while connecting to wifi

Solid red light
    Microphones are off


White Light
    You are adjusting the

    Echo's volume

## Power LED

At the top of Echo is a light called Power Led.
This will show you the wi-FI connection status to you.

1. A white light means that your device has a wi-FI connection.
2. An Orange light means there is no wi-fi connection.
3. A blinking orange light means Echo is connected to Wi-Fi but cannot access Alexa.

## Microphone Button

At the top of the Echo, you will find the microphone off button.
When you press the button then the

Echo microphones are switched off. After turning the microphone off the light of the Echo will turn to red

## Action Button

Another button at the to of the Echo is Action button this wakes Alexa.
If this button is held for five seconds then this will put Echo into wi-Fi Setup mode.
This button is also used to turn off a timer of the alarm.

## Volume Ring

Turning the volume ring clockwise, Alexa's volume will increase.
And turning the Volume ring anti – clockwise the volume will decrease.
The light ring represents the volume level.

## Bluetooth Settings

Echo has the Bluetooth connectivity property, you can connect Echo with your mobile devices.

Use the command "Pair". This will pair your Bluetooth device to Echo. Make sure the device you are connecting is in range and the Bluetooth is turned on

To disconnect command "disconnect"

## Multiple Devices

Using Alexa apps you can manage up to 12 different Alexa enabled devices.

For Echo and Echo Dot choose different wake words, if a

different device has same wake word then make sure they are at least 30 feet apart.

For Fire TV Devices and Amazon Tap give each device a different name. You can share content across different devices , content which can be shared across different devices from your Amazon account includes:

Flash briefing
Household profiles
Music & Media
Shopping
Smart Home Devices
To Do Lists

Content that cannot be shared across your Amazon account:

Alarms
Sounds

Wake Words
Bluetooth Connections

You can access all the shared content from the Alexa Apps and it will show you all the shared contents.

**Software Updates**

1. Open Alexa Apps
2. GO to left-hand side navigation menu
3. Choose "Settings"
4. Select your device
5. GO to "Device Software Version"
6. Now to download the latest software version make sure your Echo is switched on and Wi-FI is connected also stop commanding or requesting to Echo.
7. Now the light ring will turn blue

once the updates are ready to be installed.

## Chapter 2- Alexa

Alexa is a cloud-based software, this is voice recognition software.

This Alexa gets activated by the use of wake word you chose in the last chapter.

You can ask Alexa anything like

"What is the weather in New York Today?" or you can ask anything to do like

"Play Linkin Park new album".

You can also connect Alexa to the smart home devices and you can also control your thermostat, lights, power outlets by commanding the Echo.

For example, you can say

"Alexa, turn on the lights in bathroom".

you can review your voice interaction with Alexa.
1. Open Alexa Apps.
2. Choose Settings
3. Select History

You can also delete the interactions with the Alexa from your History or make corrections if necessary.

To delete any interactions simply select the entry and select "Delete"

Here is the list of questions you can ask Alexa:

"Alexa, what is the weather here tomorrow?"

"Alexa, when is Women's Day this year?"

"Alexa, what is thirteen when added with seventeen?".

"Alexa, what is the capital of England?"

"Alexa, how far is Sun?"

"Alexa, when was the world war 2 happened?"

"Alexa, who wrote Fifty Shades of Grey?"

"Alexa, what is the IMBD rating of Family Guy"?

"Alexa, how far is Los Angeles from Here?"

"Alexa, Wikepidea: "Jayden James"

## Weather Forecasts

Alexa uses AcuWeather for the weather information and it can provide you the weather information depending upon your location you live in.

To make this happen you need to set the location of your Alexa Device.

1. Open the Alexa Apps.
2. Open the navigation panel in the left.
3. Select "Settings"
4. Choose your device.
5. Select "Edit" in "Device Location"
6. Now enter the address and hit "Save"

After your location is saved you can ask Alexa anything about the weather in your location like when is the rain etc.
You can ask Alexa about the weather in other location too.

## News Updates

You can Ask by simply saying "Alexa, what is the news?"

## Traffic Updates

You can plan your journey with Alexa

get the distance information and current traffic status also.

1. Open Alexa App.
2. Open the navigation menu on the left side
3. Select"Settings"
4. Choose "traffic"
5. Select "Change address".
6. Fill in the address in the "To" and "From" section
7. Now click "Save Changes".

Now you can ask Alexa anything like:

"Alexa, what is the traffic right now?" etc.

## Calendar

With the help of Alexa you can add events to your calendar it can also

recall your events.
To do this you need to link your google calendar with the Alexa App.

Ask questions like:

"Alexa, what is on my calendar?'

"Alexa, add Go Biking with Jennifer to my calendar for Monday, October 24th at 10 am."

## Searching for the Nearby Places

Alexa uses a service "Yelp" to find services located nearby you.

Make sure your device location is correct by following

1. Open Alexa App.

2. Open the navigation menu on the left sid.
3. Select "Settings".
4. Choose Traffic"
5. Select "Change Address"
6. Fill in the "To" and "From" sections
7. Select "Save Changes"

you can ask things like

"Alexa, what is the phone number of Star bucks?"

"Alexa, what are the businesses nearby?"

"Alexa , find the nearest coffee shops". Etc.

## Setting Your Alarms and Timers

TO set or confirm alarms ask Alexa like

"Alexa, when is my alarms set for?"

"Alexa, cancel my alarm for tomorrow."

"Alexa, how much time is left is on my timer?"
etc.

you can also use Alexa to stop or snooze your alarm when it goes off.

"Alexa, stop"

"Alexa, snooze"

You can also determine the volume and tone of your timer and alarms by using Alexa apps.

1. Open Alexa App.
2. Open navigation menu on the left-hand side
3. Select "Settings"
4. Choose your device
5. Select "Sounds" and choose "alarm and timer volume".

Manage Lists

Alexa can help you to stay organized. You can manage a list of up to 100 items on each list.

To open a list

1. Open the Alexa App.
2. Go to the left-hand side navigation menu
3. Select "Shopping and To-Do Lists" and select your list and view.

You can also command Alexa to add items to your existing listing by giving the following commands:

"Alexa, what is on my To-Do List?"

"Alexa, what is on my Shopping List?"

"Alexa, put orange onto my Shopping List?"

You get an idea.
You can also mark an item as complete in Alexa by going to the "Shopping and To-Do Lists section as instructed above and simply select the checkbox next to an item.
You can also view your completed items by going to the same "Shopping and To-Do Lists" section as described in the above steps and select "View Completed".

## Smart Home Devices

You can operate numerous devices with the help of Alexa these devices include: Lights, fans, thermostats, doors, locks, power outlets and appliances.

You need to go through the instruction manual which comes with the appliance manufacturer you have before connecting your device with Alexa.

But before you need to download the companion app to connect your home appliances with the Alexa.

1. Download the companion app.
2. Use the same WiFI as Alexa and set up your device.
3. Make sure your device has latest running software,

How to connect your smart home device with Alexa:
1. Open Alexa App.
2. Open the left side navigation menu
3. Select "Skills"
4. Se;ect "Refine"
5. Choose "Smart Home Skills"
6. Search for the skill
7. Select "Enable"
8. Sign in using the login credentials which came along with the device and click "Save".
9. Now select "Discover Devices"

Now you can operate your home appliance by commanding Alexa like"

Alexa, turn on_____(your home device name)"

Alexa, turn off_____(your home device name)"
etc.

By the use of Alexa Skills Kit, you can create your own skills.
To do this:

1. Open Alexa App.
2. Open the left-hand-side navigation menu
3. Select "Skill"
4. Choose "Refine"
5. Select "Smart Home Skills"
6. Here you can define your skill.

## *Chapter 3: Music*

You can use the command to listen to music with your Echo, all you need to do is to just ask for a music to play and the rest is done for you.

You can command these things to Echo-

Adjust the volume -" Volume up/ Volume Down"

To hear details about the track currently playing -" Who is this?" or "What song is this" or "Which artist sings this?"

Play a song -" Play the song [song name]" or" Play some music"

To play an album- "Play the album [album name]"

To play music by an artist – 'Play songs by [artist name]'

To play song from a genre - "Play some [genre name] music"

To paly a playlist -"Listen to my [Paylist nane] playlist"

To paly songs that have been paused or stopped- "Play" or "Resume"

To Stop the track that is playing - "Stop" or "Pause"

To go to the next or previous track - "Next" or "Previous"

To repeat songs -"Repeat"

To look the music the music queue- "Loop"

To Shuffle songs or tracks of an album or playlist - "Shuffle and "Stop Shuffle".

## Streaming

Echo allow you to listen to streaming music services like Spotify Premium, iHeartradio, and Pandora.

To link to these music services


1. open Alexa app.
2. Open the left-hand side navigation bar.
3. Choose "Music and Books" and choose your streaming service from

the options.
4. Now select "Link account to Alexa"
5. Now sign into your account
6. Now that you have logged in into your streaming account your music service will be connected.

To unlik your account:

1.   Open Alexa Apps.
2. Open the left side navigation menu
3. Choose "Music and Books"
4. Select your streaming service and click on "Unlink"

Now you have linked your streaming service with the Alexa, you can command Alexa tp stream music:

To Play Prime Music-"Play Prime Music"

To Play SpotifyPremium - "Play SpotifyPremium"

To Paly a radio station "Pay {frequency of station}" or "Play [Station name]"

To Play a custom station "Paly my [Artist/genre] station on [Pandora/iHeartRadio/Prime Music]"

To play a podcast or program - "Play the podcast [Podcast name]/" or "Plat the program {program name}"

To skip the next song - "Skip"

To like or dislike a song "I like this song or I don't like this song" or "thumbs up" or "thumbs down"

To Take a frequency played song

off the play list- "I am tired of this song"

## Buying Music

You can shop for music but o do this you need to have a valid USA billing address and US bank or US amazon.com gift card.

To edit settings to identify whether you require a confirmation code :

1. Open Alexa app.
2. Open left hand side navigation menu
3. Select "Settings"
4. Select "Voice"
5. Choose "Purchasing"

Now you can use the following command to do shopping:

to shop for a song or album "Shop for the song [Song name]"

to shop for song by a artist name - "Shop for songs by [artist's name]"

To buy the song currently playing - "Buy this [Song/album]"

To add currently playing to your playlist-"Add this [song/album] to my library"

## Chapter 4: Shopping

You can purchase anything from Amazon.com, to do this you need to update your" voice purchasing settings"

1. Open the Alexa Apps.

2. Go to the left hand side navigation menu.

3. Choose "Settings"

4. And select "Voice Purchasing".

5. Now toggle the "Purchase by voice" to turn it on or off.

In the above settings you can also enable confirmation code, which means if the confirmation code is on then Alexa will ask you the 4 digit code before purchasing anything.

To do this

In the "Voice Purchasing " section select "Require confirmation code", supply the 4 digit confirmation code And select "Save Changes".

Now every time before purchasing they will ask you the 4 digit confirmation code.

In order to buy physical product you need to have them ordered from Amazon.com

You will also need 1 month free trial of Amazon Prime membership Commands to order items from Amazon.com are:

To add an item to your cart list "Add

[item name] to my cart

To cancel the order "Cancel my order"

To track the status of an order "Track my order"

you can also visit your Amazon.com account to manage your order.

## Final Note:

**This simple guide covers the simple way to use Echo, If you found this book helpful then you can leave a feedback on Amazon.com so that I can improve the**

*quality of this book.*

www.ingramcontent.com/pod-product-compliance
Lightning Source LLC
Chambersburg PA
CBHW071832200526
45169CB00018B/1378